CL

GULLIVER'S TRAVELS

JONATHAN SWIFT

ADAPTED BY SAVIOUR PIROTTA · ILLUSTRATED BY ALVARO FERNANDEZ

NEW BURLINGTON BOOKS

Shipwrecked

My name is Lemuel Gulliver. I am a ship's surgeon, which means I look after sick sailors while they're at sea. It's exciting travelling around the world, and you never know what's going to happen next.

Take the summer of 1699 for example. My ship was somewhere in the southern hemisphere when it got caught in a terrible storm.

The wind dashed the ship straight against a large rock and the hull was smashed to pieces. I remember being thrown headlong into the water. The waves tossed me about like a cork.

I must have floated around for hours but gradually I became aware of sand under my feet. I was close to land. The last thing I remember is crawling out of the sea on to a beach. And then I passed out…

I woke up with the sun on my face. I tried lifting my hand to shield my eyes, but I couldn't. My whole body, even my hair, was pinned to the ground. It felt like being trapped in a spider's web!

Suddenly I felt something crawling up my leg. A mouse or a spider, I thought. The creature scuttled across my stomach and came into view.

It was a man, no bigger than a toy solider. And he was armed! He held a bow and arrow pointed at my face.

Little People

For a moment I thought I was dreaming. Then I could feel hundreds of other creatures crawling all over me. I let out a loud roar, which sent them all reeling. But soon they were back. By now I was scared.

I wriggled my hand until it broke free of the ground. The little creatures had tied me with rope to little pegs in the ground. I shook my head savagely and felt my hair loosen. At last I could look around me.

There were thousands of the little people. I swatted at them with my free hand but one of them cried, *"Tolgo Phonac."*

A volley of little arrows came flying at me, sharp as needles. I cried out in pain.

"Tolgo Phonac," came the order again, and more arrows stung my face and hands.

It wasn't going to be so easy to get rid of the little people after all. I lowered my hand and lay still, thinking. The little people all around me continued to whisper. Well, it sounded like whispers to me, but they were actually talking at the top of their voices. Then one of them climbed back on to my chest.

He was unarmed, and he bowed to me politely. I smiled back, to show him I meant no harm. The little man, who I took to be an official of some sort, shouted an order. I felt my hair being loosened from the pegs, so that I could turn my head properly.

I raised my hand very slowly and pointed to my mouth with my free hand. "Food," I gasped.

The official nodded. I felt what I took to be ladders being placed against my shoulder and several men clambered on to my chest. They were carrying what for them were enormous baskets, the contents of which they tipped out close to my chin. I picked them up gently between thumb and forefinger. They were very small joints of roast meat, which I gobbled up at once.

I pointed to my lips again. "Drink. Thirsty," I said.

Smiling, the official gave another order. I heard something being rolled towards me. A barrel! I placed my hand on the ground to receive it and raised it to my parched lips. The contents tasted like nectar.

The crowd cheered wildly. My head began to spin, and I realized that the drink must have contained a sleeping potion…

While I was asleep, the little people dragged me with ropes and hooks on to a cart. They tied me to it securely, sweeping my hair under my head so it would not trail on the ground. What must have been 1500 horses were then harnessed to the vehicle, and we set off inland.

The Emperor

I had no idea what was happening, of course, but we were heading towards the main city. We travelled all day and most of the night, followed by a huge crowd.

Towards dawn, the cart stopped near a disused temple some distance from the city walls. It was just about big enough for me to crawl into, and was where I was to live.

The little people tied one end of a thick metal chain around my ankle and the other end to one of the pillars of the temple.

I was woken some time later by a loud blast of trumpets. I managed to turn my head a little and saw a wooden tower close to my face. A man stood on top of it.

He appeared to be the emperor of the people, because he wore a crown on his head. The emperor smiled at me and bowed just like the official had the day before.

All at once, the crowd rushed forward and I could feel people crawling all over me. I roared angrily and wriggled to shake them off.

The emperor on the tower shouted. Everyone backed off and soldiers came forward with swords. A moment later they had cut the ropes holding me down. I stretched my arms.

And then I stood up!

Welcome to Lilliput

A loud gasp rippled through the crowd as everyone realized just how enormous I was. There were a few screams. A lot of people fainted. I smiled at the emperor, and bowed to let him know how pleased I was to be released from the ropes, even though I was still chained to the pillar.

The emperor climbed down from the wooden tower and advanced towards me on his horse.

"Lilliput," he said, waving his arms at the landscape around us.

"Lilliput, your majesty," I repeated, to show that I understood this was the name of the country I was in.

The emperor clapped and several cooks rushed forward with steaming cauldrons on wheels. I feasted once more, on chicken and beef and cake. There was drink too, served in barrels.

While I ate, the emperor made a grand speech. I could not understand a word but he mimed a lot, so I got the meaning of what he was saying. It seemed that I was welcome in this country as long as I caused no trouble. When he finished, there was another blast of trumpets and the court followed him back to the city.

The moment the gate was shut, the crowd started edging towards me. Most people were friendly, especially the old ones and the toddlers. But a few young fellows started firing arrows, and one nearly got me in the right eye.

Immediately, some guards rushed forward to arrest six of them. The guards tied their hands behind their backs and pushed them towards me.

I picked them up one by one and dropped five in my waistcoat pocket. I held up the one that had nearly blinded me to the crowd. I took my penknife out of my pocket and brought it close to him. His eyes bulged with terror. Then I cut the ropes around his wrist and set him down on the ground.

The crowd cheered, and when I had done the same for the others, I knew that I had taken the first step towards my freedom.

Over the next few weeks, I remained chained to the pillar. The cooks continued to bring me food, and at night I crawled into the temple to sleep.

I am very good at languages, and I soon started to pick up a few words from the cooks and guards. Before long I could hold simple conversations. I learned that the emperor really liked me and saw in me the opportunity to discover more about the world beyond Lilliput's shore.

Longing to be Free

However the guards insisted I had to be careful. Most of the emperor's advisors wanted to get rid of me. Flimnap, the treasurer, claimed I would cost too much to keep. And Skyresh Bolgolam, the admiral, worried that I might turn on the people.

The emperor, though, took to paying me a daily visit. He would sit on a throne and listen to stories about my travels. Soon I felt we had become friends. I asked for the chain to be removed from around my ankle.

The emperor smiled and said, "I will set you free one day but you must first swear peace with me and my country."

"I do," I replied immediately.

"You must also allow yourself to be searched," added the emperor. "It is the custom here that anything you bring with you becomes the property of the crown."

"That is no problem, either," I said.

Two officers searched me and removed my handkerchief, my penknife and comb, my sword and pistols, a purse full of gold, a compass and a bundle of letters tied together with string.

My weapons and the purse were loaded on to a cart and taken away, but the emperor let me keep my comb, handkerchief, compass and penknife.

I also managed to keep a pair of reading glasses, which were in a secret pocket under my belt. The officers had failed to see them, and I said nothing about it. I'm glad I didn't, for soon those reading glasses would come in very handy.

Bit by bit, I started to gain the trust of the people in Lilliput. Every day, I lay out in the sun and let young couples walk all over my back as if they were strolling in the countryside. I allowed the children to play hide and seek in my long hair.

The emperor continued to visit me. Every day he arrived on a different horse, and that gave me an idea. I picked some twigs from around the temple and built a little wooden stage. The floor was my handkerchief stretched tight as a drumskin across it. I trained a few of the guards to do tricks on it with their horses.

One day when the emperor visited, we staged a grand spectacle. The horsemen acted out mock battles, attacking and retreating with great gusto. They fired blunt arrows and staged exciting swordfights.

When it was over, the emperor said to me, "After much deliberation and consideration, our parliament has decided that you have earned your freedom."

The Rules

"Here we have some rules you must agree to. Swear to live by them and you shall be free," said the emperor. Skyresh Bolgolam came forward with a scroll and read out the rules.

Rule 1: Man-Mountain (which is what they called me) *must not leave our country without permission.*
Rule 2: Man-Mountain must not enter the capital city unless ordered by the emperor.
Rule 3: Man-Mountain must not lie down in fields where he might flatten crops.
Rule 4: Man-Mountain must take care not to trample on people, horses or carriages.
Rule 5: Man-Mountain shall assist Lilliput in its war against the wicked people of Blefuscu.

I swore to keep my word by reciting a statement while holding my right foot in my left hand. Then I had to place the middle finger of my right hand on the crown of my head while holding the thumb against the tip of my right ear.

The crowd cheered, and the emperor's blacksmiths broke open the padlocks round my feet. I was free at last. That night I crawled back into the temple to sleep a happy man.

I lay in the darkness, and wondered what kind of country Blefuscu was...

Which End of the Egg?

Months passed, and I became used to living in Lilliput. Then one day the Principal Secretary of Private Affairs came to see me. His name was Reldresal.

I showed him to a small armchair and table I had just been given, but he insisted on me picking him up and holding him close to my right ear. What he had to tell me was a secret and he didn't want us to be overheard.

I learned a lot from Reldresal that day. Lilliput had been at war with the neighbouring country Blefuscu for a long time.

"How did it start?" I asked.

"A long time ago, our two countries were great allies," said Reldresal. "After all, Blefuscu is very close to Lilliput. Only a narrow channel of water separates us.

"In those days, people both in Lilliput and Blefuscu used to break open their breakfast eggs by hitting them with a teaspoon at the wider end. Then one day his present majesty's grandfather decided eggs tasted better if they were broken open at the narrower end. He passed a law saying that from then on everyone had to do the same.

"The people of Lilliput obeyed, even though they believed that our scriptures said eggs must always be broken open from the wider end. The rulers of Blefuscu, however, were most affronted.

"People in our world have been breaking open their eggs from the wider end for thousands of moons, they argued. Why should they change now at the whim of an emperor?" Reldresal continued.

"Of course, what the scriptures actually say is that people should crack their eggs open at whichever end they think fit. The trouble is, nobody bothers to read the scriptures. Our emperor's scribes have written dozens of books explaining why eggs should be broken open from the narrower end. And the professors over at Blefuscu have penned hundreds more books proving that eggs should be broken open at the wider end.

"It has led to a war that I fear Lilliput will lose. You see, some nobles in Lilliput have relatives in Blefuscu and are acting as spies for them. I'm afraid for our future, Man-Mountain. Blefuscu might be a smaller country than us but its navy is much bigger. They have more cannons too. Their ships are getting ready to sail to Lilliput as we speak. That is why his majesty asked me to talk to you. Perhaps you can help us."

I told Reldresal to tell the emperor I would not get involved in the argument. But I would do everything to protect him from his enemies.

Hero of Lilliput

The next morning, I made my way to Lilliput's northern coast and, lying hidden behind a hill, looked across the water to Blefuscu. I could see the harbour very well, and about fifty or so warships anchored there.

There were lots of smaller boats too, mostly fishing craft and sleek ferries. People were everywhere around the harbour and I guessed they were preparing to send the fleet to attack Lilliput that very next day.

Hurrying back to the city, I had the rope makers twist me fifty ropes. I asked the blacksmiths to make me fifty large hooks, which I fixed to the end of each rope. Armed with these, I returned to the north coast and waited in my hiding place until it got dark.

It was a moonless night. Taking off my shoes, I waded into the water and swam across the channel, taking the ropes and hooks with me. When I rose out of the water in the harbour, the people there went wild with fear. Those on the ships dived straight overboard. The ones on land ran screaming indoors.

I fixed a hook on to the prow of each warship. Then I twisted the fifty ropes together and, hauling them over my shoulder, started walking back out to sea.

By now, the people of Blefuscu had regained their wits and started to attack me. I could feel thousands of arrows pricking the back of my neck. And the ships wouldn't move. They were still anchored. I needed to cut the anchor ropes with my penknife.

Quickly, I reached into the secret pocket under my belt and put on my reading glasses. As I slashed the ropes, I could feel dozens of arrows bouncing against the glass lenses, but my eyes were safe.

Once out of the harbour, I slowed down a little. I could see the lights on the shores of Lilliput across the channel. The emperor and most of the country, it seemed, had turned out to watch my return. They could make out the ships, but couldn't see me in the dark.

"It's the Blefuscans," I heard someone scream. "We're done for!"

"You are safe," I shouted back. There was a tremendous cheer on the shore, which must have carried on the wind all the way to Blefuscu.

I was declared a hero. The emperor made me a knight then and there on the beach.

"From now on," he declared, "you shall be known as Sir Quinbus Flestrin, knight of Lilliput."

Peacemaker

The very next day, there was a great banquet to celebrate the victory over Blefuscu.

"You have done us proud," stated the emperor as we ate. "With your help, Sir Quinbus, we will crush the people of Blefuscu once and for all. They shall be our slaves."

"I said that I would help protect your country from harm," I replied. "But the people of Blefuscu are a free nation. I shall not be the cause of them becoming slaves to another country. Why, I have been told that before this war started the young people of Lilliput often journeyed to stay in Blefuscu. And I believe that the nobles of Blefuscu came here to learn from your scholars and witness the glory of your court. Indeed, there has always been a lot of trade between your two nations. You cannot live without one another. If you would like, your majesty, I could be your ambassador. I am sure that a visit from me, and a talk with the Emperor of Blefuscu could bring about peace."

The emperor looked pleased with my suggestion. "Of course, you shall go to Blefuscu on our behalf," he said.

As he said this I noticed Skyresh Bolgolam, the admiral, frowning at the treasurer, Flimnap. I should have known those two would cause trouble for me but I was too proud of my achievements that day to think about it for long.

The Fire

For the next couple of weeks, I busied myself building a house outside the city. It was a proper timber cottage with ceilings high enough for me to stand without bumping my head! I built myself furniture too, and bought small tables and chairs from the local carpenters for my little visitors.

A few weeks later, something happened which was to give Skyresh and Flimnap more ammunition to use against me. I was asleep, snug in my newly built bed, when I heard screaming. I threw open a window and saw an enormous crowd outside my door.

"The royal palace is on fire," someone shouted. "Can you help?"

As I approached the palace, picking my way carefully through the streets so as not to squash anyone, I could see a red light glowing in the sky above it. The empress's apartments were in flames. Smoke was pouring out of the windows.

The palace guards had filled buckets with water but it wasn't enough to stop the fire. As luck would have it, I had drunk a lot earlier that evening. So I relieved myself on the fire, putting it out in less than three minutes.

The crowd cheered, but, without knowing, I had just broken a law. It was a crime for a man to relieve himself inside the royal grounds.

The Plot

Soon after, a visitor arrived at my house, with the curtains of his carriage tightly closed. His coach driver signalled to me to lift the carriage and I placed it on my dining table.

"My master requests you close the doors and windows," said the coachman. "We should be in grave danger if any of the emperor's spies saw us here."

When the coach door was opened, I saw that my guest was none other than Reldresal.

"I came to warn you," he said. "You are in grave danger. Flimnap has been spreading nasty rumours that you are a spy. And Skyresh Bolgolam has convinced the emperor you are working for the Emperor of Blefuscu. To make matters worse, her royal highness was most offended by the way you put out the fire."

"But I only wanted to save people's lives, not to mention the palace," I cried.

"Politicians are a strange lot," said Redresal. "An order for your arrest has been given."

"What will my punishment be if I am found guilty?"

"Relieving oneself in the palace grounds could mean a year in prison. Spying and helping the enemy are considered the greatest offences in Lilliput," replied Reldresal. "If convicted, you will be sentenced to death. And you will be found guilty because Flimnap will pay criminals to lie about you," he continued gravely.

"Luckily I convinced his majesty that the death sentence was too harsh for someone who had just saved Lilliput from an invasion. 'The people will not be happy, your highness,' I said. 'He is their hero.'

"'I agree,' said the emperor. 'What do you think his punishment should be?'"

"And what did you suggest?" I asked.

"That you have arrows shot into your eyes until you are blind. It was the only suitably horrible thing that I could think of on the spot. If I hadn't come up with something gruesome, Flimnap and Bolgolam might have had their way.

"As it happens, the emperor agreed with my suggestion. Of course, no one outside the emperor's inner circle yet knows that you are going to be tried for treason.

"You are very popular with the common people in Lilliput. You will be arrested and tried in a week's time. Everything will happen extremely fast. You will be found guilty before anyone has time to leap to your defence! You must escape to Blefuscu. It's the only way...

"I have sent word to the emperor there. The Blefuscans know that you were against the Emperor of Lillliput invading their island. You will be welcomed in their country. You should set out immediately."

Escape from Lilliput

Reldresal was right. I needed to get away before it was too late. I had to be careful, though. I must not let Flimnap and Bolgolam suspect anything.

So I wrote a letter to the emperor.

Your Majesty,
Following our conversation about my journey to Blefuscu, I have set off right away. I expect negotiations will take at least a week, so please do not worry if you do not see me until then.
Your humble subject,
Quinbus Flestrin [Sir]

I placed the letter where it would be found by the first nobleman to visit in the morning. Then I packed a few belongings and crept out under the cover of darkness.

Luckily it was a moonless night. In the harbour, I selected a large ship. In it, I put the things I had brought with me, as well as my boots and jacket. Pulling it behind me, I waded out till the sea was up to my shoulders.

I waited in the channel until the sun came up, for I did not want to startle the people of Blefuscu. But by the time I reached the harbour, a great crowd had gathered.

The Emperor of Blefuscu heard of my arrival and sent two guides to show me the way to the palace. That is how, that evening, I came to dine with the Emperor of Blefuscu, whom I found charming, polite and very wise.

The Boat

I had planned to stay in Blefuscu for a while, but three days after my arrival, a true miracle happened.

I was walking along the north coast of the island, when I spotted something out at sea. It looked like an upturned boat, bobbing on the water. A small rowboat, I reckoned, but one from my part of the world. It was a vessel built for someone my size. Perhaps it had been blown here by the same winds that had carried me to Lilliput well over a year ago…

I hurried back across Blefuscu and begged the emperor to lend me twenty of the biggest ships still in his navy. He agreed, and the warships set off round the coast immediately, taking some three thousand sailors with them.

I crossed the island again on foot. The current had swept the boat closer and I could see it was really from my own world. The little ships arrived and I asked the captains of each to fix a rope to their hull. I then took the end of each rope and holding them all carefully in my hand swam out to the boat. It did not take long to pass the twenty ropes through a large hole in the front of the boat.

At my signal, the three thousand sailors all started rowing, dragging my boat behind them. By nightfall they had reached the shallows, where I could push the boat on to land with my own bare hands. At last, I had a means to escape and I was determined to get away as soon as possible.

It took me only a few days to repair the boat, using timber from fallen trees. But, before I could set off, I was summoned to see the emperor. A messenger had arrived from Lilliput. He had a letter for the Emperor of Blefuscu, written by Skyresh Bolgolam and signed by the Emperor of Lilliput in red ink. It said that I was wanted in Lilliput to stand trial for terrible crimes.

The Emperor of Lillput urged the Emperor of Blefuscu to send me back right away. In return, the people of Lilliput would start breaking their morning eggs at the same end as the people of Blefuscu. There would be peace between the two nations again.

"He also writes here," said the emperor to me, "that I must not tell you that you are to be put on trial. The poor fools do not know you know about their horrible little plot already, although they are worried you might like it here and stay indefinitely."

Goodbye to the Little People

He looked up from the letter. "You have been most kind to us, despite the theft of our navy. We shall never forget how you refused to help conquer us. If you stayed here, we would make sure you never came to any harm. All you have to do is help us in our war against Lilliput."

That would be jumping from the pan into the fire, I thought to myself. War is war whichever way you look at it, and I meant to stay out of it.

"Your majesty," I said. "I have only in these last few days found a means to return to my own world. I could never be truly happy in yours, for everyone belongs to their own people. Besides, if I were to remain here, it would be one more reason for quarrels between your two countries. I beg you to let me go."

"Perhaps you are right," replied the emperor. "If you leave tonight, I could write back to the Emperor of Lilliput and tell him you escaped. I'll also tell him that we did not stop you from doing so, because we realize that you could be as dangerous to us as you are to them."

"That's most kind of you," I answered. "The people of Lilliput believe that I fell out of the moon. You could tell them I returned to the sky."

By the time I got into my little boat the next morning, the people of Blefuscu had gathered on the shore to bid me farewell. The emperor, who arrived in his golden coach, gave me two purses full of gold.

I had already packed enough food and water for a long journey, because I did not know how long it would take me to find my own civilization again. But it was a risk I knew I had to take.

I had taken six little cows with me too, as well as a bull and two sheep. I wished I could take a few of the people with me also, for they would convince my friends back home that I had indeed been part of a fantastical adventure.

But I knew the poor creatures would be as lost in my world as I had been in theirs. So I waved farewell to everyone and started paddling out to sea, using a pair of oars that I had carved out of a tree.

I still had my compass with me but I have to confess it was not much use. I had no idea where I was or where I should be headed. I just knew that my ship had foundered somewhere not far from Van Dieman's Land in the southern hemisphere.

Blefuscu was soon out of sight! I rowed for days, using my food and water sparingly. Eventually I lost count of the days and of the little meals I had.

Rescued at Last

As the days and nights passed, my mind started to wander and I imagined I saw all sorts of weird things on the high seas – ghost ships and pirate ships and giant birds swooping over me. The sun was unbearable and I put the little animals in my coat pocket to protect them from the fierce heat.

Then early one morning I spotted a ship. A real ship! As it came closer I noticed it was flying a British flag. The sailor in the crow's nest saw me and shouted: "Man ahoy!"

I was saved at last. A boat was sent out to fetch me, with the ship's doctor in case I should need help. "Where have you come from?" asked the captain when I was safely aboard his ship.

"I was originally a ship's surgeon on board the *Antelope*," I said, "registered in Plymouth and departed for Van Dieman's Land in 1699. But this last year I have been living in a fantastic land where people are no more than six inches high. It's called…"

I heard a laugh go round the ship. "Poor soul, he must have lost his mind in the sun," someone roared.

"Aye," added someone else. "That's what lack of food and water do to a man. Reduce him to madness."

But I wasn't mad. I hadn't lost my mind. I put my hands in my pocket and felt the little animals squirming against them. There, my little pets were safe. And I knew without question that my adventures in Lilliput had been real…

About the author

Jonathan Swift was born in Dublin, Ireland in 1667. He studied at Trinity College, Dublin and then went to the court of King William III in London. He returned to Ireland and eventually became Dean of St Patrick's Cathedral in Dublin. He wrote a lot, but is best remembered as the author of *Gulliver's Travels*, which was published in 1726. Swift intended the book to make fun of the people of his day, making their arguments seem silly. He died in Dublin aged 78. He cared deeply for freedom and justice for everyone, and gave a great deal of his money to charity.

Other titles in the Classic Collection series:

Alice's Adventures in Wonderland • *Little Women*
The Three Musketeers • *Treasure Island* • *Pinocchio*
20,000 Leagues Under the Sea • *Heidi* • *The Wizard of Oz*
Robinson Crusoe • *Robin Hood* • *Tom Sawyer* • *Black Beauty*
The Secret Garden • *Anne of Green Gables* • *The Little Princess*

A NEW BURLINGTON BOOK
The Old Brewery
6 Blundell Street
London N7 9BH

QED Project Editor: Alexandra Koken
Editor: Maurice Lyon • Designer: Rachel Clark

First published in the UK in 2013 by
QED Publishing, A Quarto Group company,
230 City Road, London EC1V 2TT

www.qed-publishing.co.uk

A catalogue record for this book is available from the British Library.

ISBN 978 1 78171 351 8

Printed in China